Seven M

from God

for you, In His Love

xx

by

Sarah Parrott
with
Carl Smith-Haggett

RB
Rossendale Books

Published by Rossendale Books

11 MowgrainView, Bacup,
Rossendale, Lancashire
OL13 8EJ
England

Published in paperback 2012

ISBN: 978-1-291-08541-9

Copyright Sarah Parrott

Acknowledgements

Thank you so much to all those who helped and supported me whilst I wrote this book!

Big thanks of course go to Carl, for sharing his wonderful testimony and for his tireless energy and enthusiasm.

Also my thanks go to Reverend Patrick Beresford, Paddy, for his support in checking the theology and all his encouragement. And to Char, Lesley and Bonnie, members of the PITS Team (Prophetic Voices In Training and Support) at Charlynne Boddie Ministries, for their encouragement, prayers and advice.

And, of course, my heartfelt thanks go to my wonderful husband, Simon, for the countless times of proof reading and all his support, prayers and love. Also, thanks to my lovely children, Sam and Chloe, for all their patience and love.

Contents

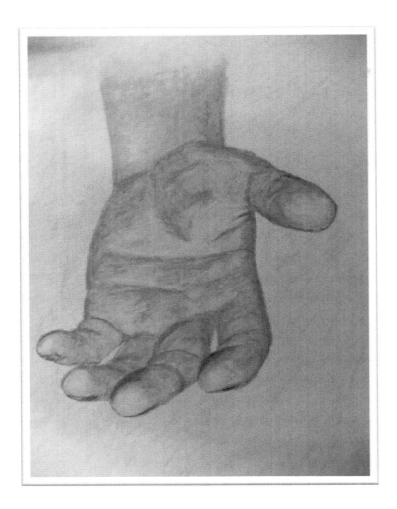

"Arise, my darling, my beautiful one, come with me."
Song of Solomon 2:10b

What are the Seven Notes about?

God is trying to connect with us. God created each one of us and loves us dearly. He longs for us to be closer to Him. He longs for us to spend time with Him. He loves it when we choose to! He is a true gentleman and will never just barge in, He will always wait to be asked.

He made each of us for a special purpose and has a wonderful plan for each of us. For me at the moment that has meant praying and listening to Him about seven different things He would like to pass on to everyone.

I have known that this should not be written by me alone, and have asked a wonderful speaker and brother in Christ, to help me by telling his story, in his own words, and share his thoughts on these aspects in each chapter.

I'll let him introduce himself;

Carl Smith-Haggett.

"I'm Carl and I'm married to Karen and we have two children Harry and Daniel.

I grew up in Brixton and Streatham in South London and come from a big family. We lived on a very rough council estate, but we loved it. I went to a church primary school but we didn't have to go to church. I used to go to Sunday school but, I remember, at no point did it ever make me say, 'Wow! This is good!'

I didn't like school too much and to be honest I was the class clown who was always making others laugh and being loud. I left school at fifteen with no qualifications.

I was in full time employment at age fifteen and to be honest I really loved it.

In 1989 when I was twenty, I started going to illegal raves all over the UK and they were great, it was then that I started to get involved in smoking weed, taking ecstasy tablets and my first adventure with cocaine.

I was both buying and selling drugs back then and drugs were to stay in my life for many, many, years.

In my twenties, I went to work for an airline company and met loads of people. It was here I met a friend. This man had been through loads of faiths and he told me, he never got nothing from them. He told me he asked loads *of questions, like I do, and did, and got no answers (like me).*

I started to read scrolls about the Bible and the Koran and I could really rip the Bible apart. I could ask questions that no one could answer and because of this I thought that I must be right. How wrong I was proved to be!

Well, my wife wanted our lad to go to a church school, and you had to go to church to get in, and I can tell you I was not happy about this at all. I didn't like churches, I found them boring and stuffy and I thought the people would be boring and stuffy as well.

I agreed to it and along we went. I did, at first, think, "What have I let myself in for?" But I met some really good people and they all accepted me for who I was, even though I could not work out why they believed what they did.

After a very short while my wife wanted to get our son baptized, and again I was not very happy. I still felt it was brain washing and hated the whole Adam and Eve story but again I agreed. The vicar came round to see us and again I pulled him apart a little, but he never minded and our son was baptized.

I went along to church for a good few years on and off and in this time I dabbled with drugs on and off and got into all sorts of things. I had scams going at every single firm I worked at and did not bat an eye lid at all.

So that's how I got to come along to St John's Church, and I spent years thinking people were mad and stupid and thinking they were wasting their time but I kept coming ....

So what changed?

A summer faith camp with my family and friends in 2010, that is what changed. It was really the last chuck of the dice to be honest, as I was about to stop going to church all together. I had no connection with God or a Jesus or anything and it made me mad.

Those of you that know me, know that I always tell it as it is. Sometimes I'm right and sometimes I'm wrong, but in my heart I don't believe that you should be something that you are not. I find a lot of people pretend just to please others. Maybe that's why it's taking me so long to get anywhere.

So here is my story and some of my experiences, and what has happened since that summer and how my faith has changed me.

I liked my life before, I guess we all do at times, but now I love my life."

We'll hear more from Carl later!

Meanwhile I'll introduce myself. I have been married to Simon for fifteen years, and we have two children, Samuel and Chloe. I am a teacher, predominantly, of adults with learning difficulties.

I have been a Christian for about 20 years. God woke me one night about four years ago and told me I needed to write a book, but that the time wasn't right yet. Since then I have trained with the 'Led By the Spirit School', with 'Charlynne Boddie Ministries', and have learnt to hear God's voice more clearly and become a member of the 'Prophetic Voices In Training and Support Team', with 'Charlynne Boddie Ministries'. Now the time is right to complete the book!

This book is made of seven chapters.

Seven things that God would like to share, with you.

Seven things that constantly trip us up, and make us falter.

Seven things we really need to let go of, let go and let God!

I have included a section of what God is saying to you, at the end of each chapter. He is talking to you, telling you what He wants you to know.

Are you ready to hear Him?

Chapter One

Worry -
No need, no point!

"Therefore I tell you, do not worry about your life, what
you will eat; or about your body, what you will wear"
Luke 12:22b NIV UK

Worry - No need, no point!

Worry! How horrible! Worry makes your tummy clench up, and your mind not focus on anything else. Worry robs us of our peace. Is it necessary though? Does it help? In a word; 'No!'

Would I like it if my children worried a lot? No! I want my children to trust that I will be there for them! It makes me wonder how I can go through life thinking and worrying about things as I often do, when I know that God is my Father! I know that all my days were planned before I was born and that all the things that happen turn out for good. So why do I worry? Why do I get myself in a state? What good can it do? I am Gods child, why do I worry?

Do any of us have experiences with worry, or fear, or feelings, especially when the mountain we know we have to climb is just a little too steep, high, uncertain , or dangerous, and we are feeling very alone? Absolutely! I know I do!

Let's hear more from Carl...

My worries have always been really stupid, really small things like going to be late for school or work. I would start racing to get there, but in reality what is going to happen? Does it really matter if we are late? Yes of course it's not good to be late, but it's far better than crashing the car or making yourself sick!

I have worried about what others have thought of me and I guess up till a short while ago I still did, but again you know that it don't do no good! After all, not everyone is going to like you, or like what you have to say, and that's fine. I made things like that, such a big thing in my head, when really it is so stupid!

I always got worked up about things that might not be done. That's both at work and home. It might be a worry about the truck not being loaded ready for me, or being late for dinner, or a friend who might let me down, and the trouble with that, is that before I am even sure that's the case, I already start to build anger and fear in myself and think about what I would do if it did happen.

Deep down, most of my real worries, have been when I've been up to no good, and as much as I hate to say it that was quite a lot! Back in the drug dealing days, I got busted quite a few times by the police and the worry then was horrid, the heart will be racing, hoping that they don't find anything. You would be thinking, "Prison is looming here," from the worry. Then the lies stem from this. You are so worried about going down, that you start to lie and lie.

I think I also worried a bit since becoming a Christian, about when I would read in church as I don't read to good. I was worried that others would laugh inside, but again what is that doing to me?

I don't worry so much now. God has my back. He knows what will happen. It's part of His plan. The Kingdom of God is all around you and you can proclaim it. It's not just about reading the Bible, it's here, now, on Earth. I can feel it!

I feel the Spirit in my body and I can tell you, it's a weird feeling, but a good feeling. We can all feel it, if we want to. It's right in front of your face! All you have to do is open the door, instead of standing next to it. I know, because I kept it wedged closed for years.

My wife, Karen and I had a picture of bikes leaning against rocks, when I was writing this. She said it was a bit like we are the bikes and Jesus is the rocks, as we need to lean on the rocks, otherwise we'll fall over! The rock won't move when the bike leans against it. It will support it.

So what are you worried about? Reach out to God and take the plunge, what have you got to lose? Face?

Shame? Fear? Evil? Well? God can deal with all the worries that you have but you need to trust Him.

Ha! There it is there it is! Why are we worrying? Why do we hide from Jesus? What do we need to do?

Invite in Jesus but mean it with all your heart and want it.

Jesus is hugging you all the time but maybe just maybe you can't feel that yet, but He is!

What is the note from God?

Matt 6:25 "Therefore I tell you, do not worry about your life, what you will eat or drink; or about your body, what you will wear. Is not life more than food, and the body more than clothes?"

Jesus was speaking to the crowd on the mountain. He had given them many instructions, and was teaching them about the life we were supposed to live. He had spoken for some while, and was near the end of His sermon on the mount, and I am sure if anyone had happened to have a smartphone, they would have been recording every word! He was speaking to a large crowd, on the mountainside. He had no audio equipment, so His voice must have been tired, but He loved His followers so much, and not wanting them to miss out, He carried on.

He wanted not just them, but future generations (like us) to know these gems of wisdom. As He was a human, himself, He was able to identify the things that get in the way of being with God. He knows that we worry about all sorts of things. He knows how much time and energy that worry takes. He sees how unhappy worry makes us. He wants us to feel relaxed. Stress does such awful things to us, doesn't it! It starts like a snowball and just gets bigger and bigger. Yet, in Matthew 6:26, Jesus says He knows what we need. He knows already. He knows and He cares for us in a very special way. He made the birds, and they are ok, and we are worth so much more to Him than birds. If we knew how much we mean to Him and walk in His ways, there would be no need to ever worry again! How amazing!

God says in the Bible, time and time again, "I will not leave you!" and in Matthew 6:25 He says that worrying about things is pretty needless! There are more important things beside the things we are worried about! Everything is just for a season (Ecclesiastes 3:1) and all things will pass away.

So why do we worry about 'stuff'? God says 'Never will I leave you, never will I forsake you' (Joshua 1:5) Joshua had received this message before, from Moses, but this was when he heard it for himself from God. Joshua was about to really stir things up and knew he had to face what seemed like an impossible battle.

He was commanded and encouraged to be strong and brave. Why? Because God was with him, going before him to make sure the plans that had been crafted so long before Joshua's birth came into action. God says this again and again throughout the Bible, that His plans will come to pass and His Will, will be done, and that it is all for good, for love. He tells us that, "Surely I am with you always' (Matthew 28:20.)

In John 1:1, Jesus is referred to as the Word, being with God and being completely God. In

John 1:14, it says that He was also completely man. The gospel of Matthew refers to Old Testament prophecies now fulfilled in Jesus, affirming him as the Messiah. I find this wonderful, that the Messiah could care so much that humans spend so much time worrying! He lets us know that worry is really bad for your health!

In Matthew 8:23-27, we find that Jesus was able to sleep through the storm, resting in God's presence! How I would love to sleep through the storms in my life! At least if I could relax and rest in His presence, through each storm, I would cope better! His disciples in the boat, though, handle the storm similarly to how I handle storms, and well, panic! They turned to Jesus in a flap and woke him. They told Him what was going on and He commanded peace, not just for the disciples, but also for the storm. He commanded the wind and the waves to stop causing problems, and they did. The disciples were amazed! Whenever I have turned to God in a crisis, He has always come through for me. The wind and the waves have become less daunting and I have had much more peace. But I do have to really concentrate on God, rather than my problems.

When I worry, it tends to make me forget all the other things I could and should be thinking about. Things I could and should be doing. I start to feel bad inside, sometimes I can't sleep. When I worry, I often crave and then choose food and drinks that are not exactly the healthiest, and then start fretting about that decision too and feel worse! When I am worried, I might snap at someone I love, or not give them the attention that they deserve and end up feeling really bad about that too and question my capabilities as a mum, wife, sister, daughter, friend etc.

If I am worrying about something, I might not concentrate fully at work, or just do the minimum to get by, and then feel guilty about it. When I worry, I feel so tired! Accidents most often happen to me at this time. I forget things at lot, as well, when I worry. I forget to make an important phone call, pay a bill, sign a letter for school, loose my keys, or forget things when I

am doing the shopping, and then have to go back
and do it again later.

I often feel less like reading the Bible too, when
I am really worried and stressed because of my
worry. At times I feel so worried I can't even
pray. I have even felt ill with worry. How silly! If
you think about it, a worry isn't about something
that will definitely happen, it's something that
might not happen! How silly of me to ever worry
then, if the event in question, that I am getting
so worked up about, might not even happen!

For me personally one worry often leads to
another until they become all consuming leaving
no room for anything else! When Jesus was
talking to his followers on the mountain, during
the Sermon on the Mount, He was trying to say,
"I have you. I am with you. I am watching your
back. I know what you need to have, or do. I
know what you want to happen. I love you.
Ultimately I know what's best for you all. I will
always be there. Trust me."

That's so comforting!! God knows what we need!
He wants us to leave it all to Him. He wants us to

live in His kingdom, not live with all these worries as the world expects us to.

Suddenly we have a choice! We don't have to worry! We can tell God in prayer and remember that God loves us and has our best interests at heart.

We are told in the Bible that Jesus was tempted in the desert, (Matthew 4,) He knew that this would happen, yet Jesus wasn't worried about how He would cope, or what would happen next or what His friends would think. He didn't go and eat a load of chocolate, or call all His friends to the pub to discuss the problem over a pint. The Bible says that He simply relied on His Heavenly Father, and His Word. And did He come through for Him? Yes! Therefore, we should trust that He will come through for us!

Isn't that great! We don't need to worry!

Not another worry, ever! There's no need! There's no point!

The note from God says,

"Please don't waste yourselves worrying. I know that things concern you, and I know that things don't always seem clear. But please remember, I am on your side. I am with you in all things. Yes, all things! Every little thing you do is noticed and watched over by Me. Every little thing that concerns you is My concern too. The difference is, that I know the outcome. It's not for you to worry about the outcomes, or the problems. Put your trust in Me and I will not fail you. I will guide you through everything. It will all work out in the end for good. You'll see. There are consequences to your actions, but even when you have made a bad choice, I will help you learn from it and move on. I will help good come through in the end. There is no need to worry about 'stuff', I know the things you need and I will provide for you. Sometimes the things you think you need, are not really what you need. I am your loving Father. I do know what is right for you and I will provide it. Stop tormenting yourselves, relax and give the problems to Me. I WILL always be there, no matter what, and I will always help you.

All things will pass away, and changes will
take place. But I will not change, EVER. I will
always love you and I will always be there for
you. Always. Let Me prove to you, that I am
trustworthy. You will feel My Peace when you
do. I love you. I will not harm you. I already
know what will happen and I have already
worked it out for Good. Nothing surprises Me.
I already know, so trust in Me, I really can
help! Do not fear, just take a deep breath,
close your eyes and focus on Me. I will always
come through for you. You will see it in the
end."

Chapter Two

God has good plans for us,
we just might not see the
whole picture yet!

"Your eyes saw my unformed body;
all the days ordained for me were written in your book
before one of them came to be"
Psalm 139:16

God has good plans, we just might not see the whole picture yet

Does God have plans? Are they good? Always? Why don't I know what the plans are then?

I started thinking about this, as a parent. Would I let my children know everything I am thinking? No, probably not! They might be too young to understand, or the time just isn't right. So why do I panic when I don't know the whole plan that God has for me?!

I used to love dot-to-dot puzzles, I loved starting at the first dot and looking for the next number, step by step until the picture could be seen. Sometimes, I could guess what the picture was going to be, and that was ok, but not nearly as much fun and as satisfying as when I didn't know! God seems to understand this and will show me just the next dot, but only when I have finished with the previous one. I have no idea how many dots there are, or when I am expected to finish, but I know that when I finish, the picture all will become clear!

Over to Carl...

For years I used to go round in circles and, of course, at the time I thought, "This is fun!" I helped myself to whatever I wanted, without a care of anyone else. "Who cares who I hurt," I thought. The same circle over and over and not even knowing what was going on. Doing bad things and not even knowing that they was wrong, accepting that it was ok. What was I doing? What was I thinking?

It became so normal to steal and do drugs, that, I didn't even blink a eye lid and became lost, so lost that it was normal and everyone else was wrong not to be like me. What was I doing? What was I thinking? Why couldn't I see what I was doing?

How do we know what we are meant to be doing? It can take years to have the answer to that but you have to, one; trust God and second; trust yourself. God has a plan. As for me, I gave up twenty three years of truck driving to teach people to drive. When I first started the training for this, I was not a Christian and my attitude was bad, but just knew I had to do it. I wasn't going to make it, but, as I will explain later, I gave my heart to Jesus, after a long struggle with God, and I started to teach. Even now, I sometimes ask "Am I meant to be doing this?" Each time I ask, I find a pupil in my car asking about God, or another pupil may call me. Sometimes I wonder where they are coming from!

Does God have a plan for me? I used to think not! We can easily switch away from His plan but open your heart and mind, and God will show you a path. The trouble is, you may not like it and it may not be 100% clear, but it is there.

When I first started to teach people to drive, work was hard to come by and I was teaching when I could and driving coaches all night at the airport (that was tough) but God had a plan for me. I know that now, even if I don't understand it sometimes!

There was two lovely Christian drivers there and they were so nice, but all the blokes (and they was rough) would mock them. I wondered why this was at first. They both spoke to me and they was shocked, that this tattooed loud mouth, had a story to tell. I never hid it, and word got round that the nutter was a Bible Basher (well that's how they said it). It was one nasty, snowy and icy night that the Good News came around... There I was at 2am in the morning with three hard core, butch men, digging cars out and defrosting cars when the comment came.

"So you're one of them then?"

I remember it well! I laughed, "Yeah, one of them!" I said, "What's one of them?"

"A Jesus nut", said the old man.

"No," I said, "I'm just me."

"So what's your story then?" I was asked, and that's not the first time I've been asked that! I could have pushed it away and hid, but why should we hide the Good News? We have the choice to hide or to tell and I choose to tell.

"Well, it's a bit like this," I said, "I used to be a thief, a thug, a drug dealer, a drug user and over all, a bit of a horrid bloke. But that's all changed now…"

I told them about how I was and the books I used to read and about church and my story. I told them how giving your life to Jesus, God and the Holy Spirit, can turn your whole life around.

*I was greeted by smiling and laughter. It was then that the old boy told me about the two Christians that worked there and how they would both say to everyone, they **need** and **have** to follow Jesus, as it is everything. Whilst I understand this is a bit correct, this was the reason why they was pushed away by the other workers. They felt it was being rammed down their necks.*

Then there it was out of the blue. The old boy said to me, "So what's so good then about it all?" He then said, "Ok, tell me about Adam and Eve."

I smiled at him and said, "Can't tell you about that, as I wasn't there!"

He asked me to tell him about Noah and the floods, and again I said, "I don't know about that, as I was not there either!" He carried on with the same line getting more and more, angry.

It was then that I said "Listen!" (Really nicely, I must add) "I can't tell you about the Bible, because first of all, I have not read it all, and second, I was not there, so I don't know what happened. But I can tell you about me".

"Ok," he said, "Tell me!"

"Are you sure?" I said.

"Yes," he said. And that was it, I was being invited to talk about Jesus and my path.

I spent about a good two hours talking of things that had happened to me. It was great that these men were really interested in what I had to say. It never made me feel good and to be honest it never does, you know I don't mean that in bad way, but I always feel like a idiot and that I'm there to be laughed at and people do, but lucky for me, I've got big shoulders so I can take it!

That evening was really great and the old boy turned round and said, "Thank you. I respect you." The reason *he said that, was because I spoke of what had happened to me and not because I wanted to ram him with God stuff.*

The kingdom of God is for everyone, but not everyone wants to hear it. I never used to want to hear it either and I have a rule that I only tell people about it if they ask, so that way I feel invited. I've only broken that rule once, and it was last year. I felt sick afterwards but that's another story! Some want to hear and some don't and some are ready and some are not.

I'm not really sure what Gods whole plans are for me and I have been asking, lots, "Lead me and guide me!" but I'm a bit slow at working it out, or maybe, hopefully, I'm doing it!

As I'm told many times I'm a mouth and I talk of God and how my life has changed and is still changing so maybe I'm to be used for talking or maybe not. Often people just come up to me, out the blue and ask me to talk about God! Some come with questions, and some come with tears! I don't know how or why they come to me, but they do! Weird!

So what is God's plan for me? At the moment, it's to tell others about Him! To show the way to Him, however I can. To tell it straight, and that's what I'm doing!

What is the note from God?

Jeremiah 29:11 "For I know the plans I have for you,' declares the LORD, 'plans to prosper you and not to harm you, plans to give you hope and a future."

I love this verse! It is so comforting isn't it! Jeremiah was writing to the Jews who were being taken to Babylonia (a prospect they were not exactly relishing!) God gave Jeremiah the right words to say at the right time. He told them that it was all going to be fine. It might look bad, but it was all under control. They had not been forgotten, it was going to work out well in the end. They would be happy. God already knew this was going to happen. He already knew how He would work it out for good.

He wanted to reassure the Jews that there were good things to come. He wanted to reassure them of His love for them, and His care of them meant that they didn't have to worry. It would all be OK. Isn't that lovely? God cared enough to let them know that everything would work out well. And that they would prosper and have a future.

I sometimes wonder if I'm doing the right things, in the way I'm supposed to be doing them or maybe it's time to move on to the next step in my life. I can feel so distant from God in times of hardship, and wonder why God is letting me go through this, but then a few days, weeks, or even years later, something might crop up which makes those things I went through help! So, then, I can really see the bad turning into something good!

If we look at some of the great people from the bible, we see that God didn't necessarily tell them the whole plan at the start, but expected them to follow one instruction at a time, for example in Genesis 22:1-15, we are told about the time God asked Abraham to sacrifice his long awaited son. Abraham followed all the instructions, with what must have been tears and fear, and found the outcome of that wonderful plan, just before he was about to sacrifice his baby boy, and Isaac grew up to father future generations.

When I am wondering what the next step for me is, I tend to flounder around a fair bit! I ask my husband, then my friends and family what they think I should do and then spend a lot of time wondering myself. It might be more beneficial next time to just ask God what my next step should be! Then, I might find the answer quicker!!

Sometimes I wonder why I am being led to go to a certain place, see a person, take a job, move house, etc and wonder how that can fit into any plan, but God is more amazing than I give Him credit for sometimes! Just think about it, look at 9/11, all those people who missed the bus into work that day, all the people who got held up for just a few minutes extra, that part of the plan saved their lives! I know, sadly, a lot of people did make it to work that day and did lose their lives, and that I don't have an answer for yet. Maybe I never will, but we'll look at pain and suffering in another chapter.

However, just think of the stories you have heard, or you may have some stories to tell. One of my favourites, and I can't remember where I heard it, is of a man who followed a woman home after she got petrol, when he saw someone sneak into the back of her car. He saved her life that day. He followed her home and when she asked him what was going on (as she was, understandably, rather freaked out!) he told her that someone had got into her car. The man inside the car was arrested and there was a happy ending. But suppose that man had decided to wait until the following morning to get petrol? Suppose he had forgotten his wallet and had to return home? Suppose he had checked his watch at the crucial time, and missed seeing the man sneaking into her car? Suppose his tank just didn't need filling? I am pretty sure that the woman was very glad none of those things happened! Perhaps he just had a nagging feeling to stop there for petrol. Maybe that was God keeping her safe? I am certain that anyone waiting for this man at home must have wondered where he was when he took so long, but I would imagine that they understood when they heard! So maybe that wasn't the plan for that mans whole entire life, or maybe it was? Maybe it was the plan for the woman to start a campaign getting people to lock their car doors when they go to pay for petrol? I just don't know, but one thing I do know, is that God has a good plan for me, and for every one of his children. He wants to see them whole and loved. We are all so special to him.

A while ago I had a secret plan for my children to make them feel special. I thought they needed a nice treat. Whilst they were at school I found their bucket and spade, packed their beach clothes and made up a packed tea full of all their favourite foods. I picked them up from school and, instead of driving them home, I started off towards the coast! They were very surprised and had no idea where they were going, and I just smiled and said they'd soon see! As we got closer to the beach, they were beside themselves with excitement and their faces were all lit up.

I gave them a clue and told them to look inside the bag, where they found their tea! They were very excited to see their favourite foods, but they still had no idea where they were going! As they got closer to the beach they asked lots of questions and then they saw the sea! "We're going to the beach!" they shrieked, and I couldn't stop grinning! I love seeing them that happy! They had no idea where they were going, it wasn't where they expected to be, but they loved it! Often I think I should be more like them! We are all on a journey. We are all heading towards home. What adventures lie before us, we just don't know, but perhaps, just as my children trusted that I would keep them safe and have a good plan for them, we should trust that our Heavenly Father knows what is best for us and has a good plan for us. It made me so happy to see my children's faces like that! I wonder if that's how God feels when we trust Him and follow His plans for us?

The note from God says,

"I do have good plans for you! I created each of you for a specific reason. I want each one of you to achieve a goal. I will always help you to do this and I will guide you in the easiest way. It's up to you whether you follow this path. It might be difficult sometimes, and you might not be able to see around every corner, but remember, I am here helping you

every step of the way. You are on a journey and you know the destination. You can look around you on the way or you can stare at the ground, or at where you've just been. It's up to you how much you choose to see and experience on the way. My purposes for you are always good, even though it might not feel like that at the time. I always have love in the centre of everything I do. Trust Me! It will all work out in the end, I promise. I will not leave you and I will not fail you. When you reach home, you will know all you need to know. Until then, I give you all you need. Just follow Me, one step at a time. I am always here. Loving you. My plans for you, My child, are good."

Chapter Three

Be still! You who have ears,
listen.

"He says, 'Be still and know that I am God."
Psalm 46:10a NIV UK

Be still! You, who have ears, listen!

God really cares about each one of us. He made us for a special purpose and He wants to have a relationship with us. So why do we struggle to hear God? Why don't we take enough time to listen? Why do we think it's ok to belt out a quick prayer when we need something and then move on to the next thing as fast as we can? Life can get extremely busy, cant it! Too many demands and not enough of the person to go around! We try and live at one hundred miles an hour, but this isn't what God wanted!

Would I like it if my children came to me and had chatted at top speed and then ran off before I had a chance to respond? Definitely not! How would I feel if they just sent the odd text message now and then and never replied to mine? What if they stopped making time to look at me smiling at them and smile back? I think it would hurt!

If I am God's child, then, why do I rattle out a quick prayer and then run on to the next thing? How can I expect God to talk to me when I don't give Him time? He is longing to talk to each one of us. He loves spending time with us and He loves it when we just sit with Him, basking in His presence.

Let's hear the next part of Carl's story....

I used to think that I can't hear God at all, but what in fact what was I trying to hear? What does His voice sound like? A loud deep voice that says, "I am God"? Really? It aint gonna happen like that (well for a few maybe)! God speaks in many ways, for example, through others and through pictures.

Just after I become a Christian, in fact two days later, I was driving to work at 3am. I drove to work talking to what I thought was God and was really asking Him to be clear as at that time I thought I was going nuts! I said to God "How do I know you are there?" At that moment, I was prompted to turn on the radio and the words were, "I guess you will have to trust the word of the Lord." Let me tell you, that freaked me out big time! Was God talking to me? Yes! Via a radio! So I never got God's own voice, but an audio voice through a radio!

Then on to the Monday morning and back to work, I got in my car at 4am and put the radio on to a sport talk. I drove along and thought, "Right, let's have a chat" even though I thought, "Can I do this?" It was like something said, "Well turn the radio off." I turned it off and out loud said, "Ok, listen, God. I'm not too good at all this stuff, but You know I'm trying and doing things I never have done before."

I said, "Listen, I know I can take this just for me and be selfish, but if You want me to do things, then You gotta help me. I gotta know what I'm talking about before I can pass it on." It was then I turned the radio back on and the next words were, "I guess we got to accept the words of the Lord."

I tell you what, I nearly wet myself! I laughed loud and smiled. You know, I always said, "Send an angel down and I'll believe it!" but I was getting a voice on the radio.

I turned the radio off and asked for more, I know, I'm greedy!

I turned the radio back on and the words of the bloke talking was "We can empower people to change by asking people to come forward..."

Now that sounds mad and if anyone had told me that it would happen, I would have said, "Yeah right, mad man!" I'm a lot of things, but not crazy or a story teller!

The story on the radio was about the House of Lords, so yes, those words would have been said, but to be said at those moments is something else!

A couple of years ago I was really asking God for help with my patience. I was bad. I had road rage and bad anger. I asked a lot, again and again, but God never just clicked His fingers and said "Here mate have a bit of patience," No! He made me be a driving instructor and boy did I learn patience!

The next time you pray for something, just remember, God hears you, but do you really hear God? And do you really want what He wants for you?

He will answer you. Always. Just listen to that still small voice. Wait and He will answer.

I used to drive to work taunting God and Jesus to do things; to make the sky light up and do tricks. But now, I talk to them like they are my brothers and well, they are my brothers I guess, and they talk back, it's just sometimes I don't hear it all, but I'm getting there. I ask them to help me be calm and to help others, I say out loud, "Let's see how many people we can make happy today."

I would drive along in my own world, feeling nothing really and now I drive along and when I'm talking, I get to feel a presence and I'm not worried by this, but I would have been before.

I don't hear God everyday but I do talk to Him every day, maybe I just don't get the answers right away!
God don't stop talking to us, we stop talking to Him and my wife told me that once, I said to her, "Gods not been there lately." So she said, "When did you stop talking to Him?"

God talks to us in many ways, I've had words, pictures and voices. For me at the moment it's the feeling inside. I can feel the Spirit on me and, as crazy as it sounds, it's wicked! Like all your hairs stand on end and a light wind!

I know that I need to get in to the Bible more and that I need to pray more and I know the more you give out the more you get back, so it's up to you, how much you want to listen.

What is the note from God?
Mark 7:14 "Again Jesus called the crowd to him and said, 'Listen to me, everyone, and understand this."

Here Jesus says to listen to Him. He says listen and understand. The word of God is alive and spot on! It's sharper than a double edged sword (Hebrews 4:12) Therefore, it makes sense to listen!

It strikes me that sometimes I don't really listen to people! Sometimes when I have the schedule of each family member in my head, at the same time as cooking dinner, thinking about work, and making a shopping list, I really don't focus on what people are saying to me, even my own children! They chatter on and I tune out, thinking about all the other things I have to do, then I suddenly tune in again, when there is a pause! Then I have to come clean and admit to them, "Actually, I'm sorry, I didn't get that last bit!" At which point there is usually a roll of their eyes and they start again, this time with me listening properly!

This admission is definitely not something of which I am proud! The thing is though, because I didn't listen, I didn't actually understand what they said. That is really sad, as mostly they were telling me whatever it was, because they wanted to share it with me. Why did I not care enough to concentrate on what they were saying? I found myself doing this a lot, particularly when my children were small. They would get verbal diarrhoea and I would just stop listening! How sad!

I turned round once when my daughter was chattering away, to find her intently studying my back view with a puzzled and a little down cast face, as she chatted, on and on and I washed up. I immediately felt guilty and stopped, bent down to her and listened. I smiled and nodded and was able to contribute to her chatter, and she seemed to brighten even more, and guess what? I had responded in the right places, without her feeling the need to repeat everything and she was satisfied, very quickly and moved off to more play much more happily and I finished the washing up with a smile myself!

Now I'm not saying that I manage that every time; there are times when the chores just have to be done! But I do always try and at least explain that I am listening, but have to look at what I'm doing, or say when my poor brain is on over load and just needs a couple of minutes, before I can concentrate! This seems to work quite well at the moment, although we haven't hit the teenage years yet, so I guess time will tell! Anyway, this did get me to thinking about this verse.

God wants us to listen. He wants us to listen and understand him. So do I stop long enough to listen to him? Or do I just carry on with all the lists of things to do, that clutter up my mind? I know from my job as a teacher, how frustrating it is to give an instruction, or explain an activity, and have people talk over me, or daydream and then ask me later what they were supposed to be doing. Why would I do that to God? I thank Him often and ask enough of Him during my prayer time, but do I spend enough time listening?

The psalmist expresses God's frustration in Psalm 82, where he talks about all the things He could do to help His people if only they would listen!

Proverbs 8 tells us that we can be wise if we listen to God, as with the listening, comes wisdom. In verse 32, it says our ways will be blessed if we listen to Him! So how many more reasons do we need?

If I was in any doubt, though, that God wants us to listen to Him, we hear it from His own voice, in Matthew 7:14, after Jesus was baptised, Gods voice from heaven says "This is my son, whom I love; with him I am well pleased. Listen to him." Wow! That must have been amazing to be in that crowd and hear God's heavenly voice for my own ears! I am so thankful for the all the writers of the Bible, who clearly did listen to God, so that I can read His Word all these years later!

I am astounded how often God speaks to me in different ways at different times! If I am in the car, He might speak through the words of a song on the radio, that strikes a chord in me, as if it's speaking straight to my heart, and I know those words, just then, are for me.

He might speak though another person, who happens to show up with the right words, or even just a hug or cup of coffee just when I need it most. He might speak to me through nature, where I notice how blue the sky is, or see a rainbow and marvel at the colours or a butterfly and wonder at its delicacy. I might see tall trees or the sea and feel the awesomeness of God.

He speaks to me through my thoughts, I hear a small voice, in my head, quietly telling me what I need to hear. I might have a dream, that feels very real, and feels very important. I might see a picture, or even a short movie, in my head.

He speaks to me through paintings and drawings too. Sometimes when I pray I paint or draw at the same time, and it helps me focus on God, and sometimes I will find that I have painted a picture that gives me a message, or clue, or a feeling about the prayer I prayed. Sometimes the paintings can mean different things to other people too. I have included some of these pictures to accompany each chapter. Each one was drawn or painted in prayer.

Of course, God speaks to me through the Bible as well. A verse might stick out, and the words might be quite poignant, or will stay with me and I will pray about them. The Bible is alive! Jesus often is referred to as the Word, and it says that the word is alive and sharper than a two edged sword. (Hebrews 4:12)

Occasionally I have even heard an angel speak God's message! One day when both my children were very poorly, I was praying for my daughter as she slept, desperate for us all to sleep well, as

I was getting more and more exhausted. I prayed for an angel to be with her, as I slept, and I heard, sort of in my head I suppose, "I've got it from here!" and felt an amazing peace. I immediately filled with tears and was about to pray over my son in the same way, and felt, rather than heard, a smile and I knew then that they were going to be ok for the night and that it wasn't up to me, God had them covered and was watching over His children with love. We all slept well that night.

So if Jesus cares enough about me to find all these and many more ways to talk to me, surely the least I can do is concentrate and listen, so that I can understand what He is saying. Why do we complain that God doesn't talk to us, and claim He is distant and uncaring, when actually it is us at fault, just carrying on with our busy lives, belting out the odd prayer when we need or want something, rather than taking time to have a relationship with Him and actually listen to what He says. Show Him we care by listening to

Him, and being patient. Sometimes the answer
we want, is not the answer He needs to give us.
Sometimes I think He just wants us to trust Him
and be patient. The more we get used to
listening to God, the easier we'll find it!

The note from God says,

"If you listen I will talk to you! I talk to you
all the time! You are My darling child and I
love to share things with you! I want to tell
you secrets and I want to chat for hours. I
don't hide things that you need to know. I
want to tell you things that will help you at
the right time. Will you listen to Me? Will you
hear My words and understand? I speak in
the way that is right for just you. It is
different for everyone, as there is no one like
you. There is no one like you and I talk to
you in a way that you will understand. I speak
in so many different ways. Just quiet yourself
and you WILL hear Me! Take some time, and
you will learn to hear Me. It might be that it

sounds like your own thoughts, but if My word backs it up and it is kind, then it is Me! Listen, My child, I am here and I want to talk to you."

Chapter Four

Dealing with pain.

Sin and the spiritual battle.

"For God so loved the world that he gave his one and only Son, that whoever believes in him shall not perish but have eternal life." John 3:16 NIV UK

Dealing with pain. Sin and the spiritual battle.

Pain is a problem that, in my experience, many people struggle with. Why does God allow suffering? Why did this tragedy happen to this person? Why is this happening to me? Is God punishing me? Why doesn't God love me enough to stop it? The truth is, I don't have all the answers. But for me, when I don't have the answers I go straight to the Bible. As we heard in the previous chapter, that's where wisdom comes from!

Would I like to watch my children go through something bad, something that hurt them, something sad? No way! Does God like watching me, His child feel sad? No way! Then why does He let it happen? The answer God keeps leading me to, is complicated. It has to do with the world hurting because of sin.

God did not want that to happen, yet He knew it would. He created it, and us, anyway because He loves us and He knew that some of His children would come back to Him. He loves us all so much.

It also has to do with plans that I am not yet ready to understand.

I may never be ready. But I know that one day, in heaven, I will see the wonderful outcome, where all pain is gone, and there are no more tears. I feel reassured that He will wipe away every tear I cry. (Revelation 21:4) Every single one! He promises there will be no more pain.

It comforts me to know that when I see Him face to face, He will wipe every tear from my eyes, and take away the pain, just like a loving parent. So although pain is something that makes me feel sad and something I can't fully understand, I know that God loves each one of us and cares what happens to us. He feels sad when we go through tough times, and He carries us through, even though we might not know it. He is there, through it all, loving us.

Back to Carl....

I've had different types of pain. I've broken bones before and hurt myself, but I can deal with that, I think the worst pain for me has been the mental pain and most of that, has been caused by doing stupid things and then crying out later, "Why? Why? Why?" The torment after doing drugs and then the next day saying, "I'm not going to do that again." Then beating yourself up about it. It's torture!

It's funny as, before I was a Christian and trying to get to know God, I'd make stupid promises like, "I swear God, I'm not going to do that again!" but then the fall and then the excuses would follow.

I couldn't see God in my pain as I was never looking for Him, but I know He is there now, as I feel it. That makes me feel sad, as I'm not just upsetting or hurting myself, but God too.

Sometimes we have lessons to learn from our pain, when my Mum died, I was bitter and hated God, (even though I never believed in one!) "Why?" I would ask, "Why not answer my wife's prayers for her?" But maybe He did, after all I can't see her no more but there is no more pain for her now.

Now I pray for others, for healing and I've prayed for healing with people at work and at home. It makes me feel little sometimes and scared and I think, "What am I doing?" But when you get told that the prayer helped, then you know it works.

An example of this is when I was at a pub in London, a few weeks ago, the man there, who is lovely, was worried about his head. He told me he had to go to the hospital and was worried, I said, "We should pray for it", and he said, "Yes." I was worried and I didn't really think he would say yes. The following week I asked how it was and he said "A bit better." So I said, "Let's do it again!" and we did.

Also my wife Karen has had a really bad shoulder, so bad that she has been getting treatment. She said we should pray for it, and even with Karen, I felt weird doing it, but I did. The next morning in my car, I was chatting to God and brother Jesus when I got a bit mad, asking them to help (when I get like that, stuff happens!) To my shock, that afternoon, Karen said it felt easier! So the next night we done it again. I came home from work and she is swinging that arm! Yep, even I'm a bit taken back, but I've been asking God to install me with the power to heal through me and why shouldn't He. Before I would just ask to be greedy and now I ask to help the needy.

What is the note from God?

Romans 8:22 "We know that the whole creation has been groaning as in the pains of childbirth right up to the present time."

God created us to have a deep relationship with Him. He knew we were going to mess up, and He thought we were worth it anyway. He created man, and man messed up as He knew we would. He had to banish Adam and Eve from the Garden where He would walk and talk freely and openly with them every day. That snake and the choices Adam and Eve made, ruined it. But as God knew that would happen He already had a plan. He already knew He would send His son to save us.

He would like us to want to love Him of our own accord, as I don't want to force my children to love me, I want them to choose to love me. He let us be for a long while, making that choice. Some people did return His love, and He blessed those people. You can read about them all in the Old Testament. However, there were lots of people who just didn't want to know and made choices to hurt others.

God believes in free will, and gives each of us the gift of making our own choices. Sometimes those choices affect someone else. Look at Cain and Abel as the first example, (their story can be found in Genesis.) God loved them both, yet Cain became so jealous, that he killed Abel. Yes, he felt bad afterwards, but the damage was done. What kind of a parent would God be if He didn't at least sit him on the naughty step? He banished Cain.

The cold hard truth is that sometimes people choose to hurt other people. It doesn't make it right and I am pretty sure God weeps with us, but He loves us enough to let us make those choices, and is there to help us pick up the pieces afterwards, whether that means healing them as well as their friends and family physically, as well as emotionally, as a loving parent does when their children get into a fight, or are bullied. They will be there for their child with plasters and a cuddle, feeling their child's pain

Sometimes there is another reason for pain. We might not know it at the time, but eventually it may become apparent. Let's look at the story of Joseph, in the book of Genesis. His pain seems to be part of Gods plan. He is able to hear God, but starts to boast about this. His brothers get jealous (jealousy is horrible isn't it!) and they sell him. He is locked away for a crime he didn't commit, but still listens to God and God listens to him. He is discharged from jail and becomes a powerful man, able even to save his whole family, as well as a whole country of people from starvation, including our ancestors.

Sometimes it's not just physical pain. If we go back a little further in the bible, we find Noah. He was asked to build a huge boat, with his family. How his mates must have jeered at him! They may have laughed, saying "A flood! Never! Not on that scale! You're out in the sun too much! Let's ignore him!" How upsetting that would have been! How sad for Noah, knowing that he did indeed have it right and knowing that the people around him, except for his family, thought so badly of him. How sad it must have been when they did finally understand what was happening and beg to come aboard. Listening to their screams for mercy can't exactly have been the highlight of Noah's life, yet he kept on trusting God, who was with him every step of the way.

I have seen examples of self inflicted pain in the Bible too. Let's look at David, you can read about him in the books of Samuel. He was a man who was so close to God. A man who, loved God so deeply, and listened to Him so carefully. Well what did he do? He had an affair with another mans wife, got her pregnant, and had the man murdered, making it look like an accident! Well if that wasn't asking for trouble I don't know what was! God took his baby to heaven to be with Him and the pain David felt was immense. But he turned to God, and God was there for him through his suffering, but did not change His mind. He was there for him every second, every minute, every day, and then David felt better. He continued with his life. Things got better.

But what about things that happen like earthquakes, sickness, or the death of someone young? Romans 8:22, says that the "earth is groaning". We have so much sin in the world that bad things happen. As well as people hurting one another, there are so many people who don't live by Gods ways of love, whether that's using the chemicals unwisely for the earth, using the Earth's resources unwisely, creating diseases or dangerous substances to hurt people, being greedy for money, power, fame and selfish success. I think just stress on its own can cause serious illness! Earth is a delicate balance, and sometimes, due to circumstances, that balance is out and a disaster happens. Who is the author of pain and destruction? Satan.

There is a spiritual battle raging, all around us. If you know the Star Wars films, we're on the last film now! The emperor, or in our case, Satan, is at his worst. Life is hard for a lot of people. He is working through his army, especially Darth Vader. But we can sense as we watch, that good will triumph. We know Luke Skywalker will win led by his friend Obi-Wan, his teacher Yoda, and the Force of goodness.

The battle is intense and many find out about the force of good and evil. Many choose which side they are on, and good will win, even the darkest Darth Vader, can return to good! The battle is won. The Emperor is destroyed forever. And a party commences! No more suffering! No more pain! The battle is won! Jesus confirms this through the gospel of John, chapter 16, verse33. He says "In this world you will have trouble, but take heart, I have overcome the world!"

Jesus knew pain and suffering. He knew emotional pain, He knew rejection, He knew the loss of someone He loved, He knew physical pain and He knew fear. Yet He chose to accept all that for us! He knew He would have to face it before He came to earth and He chose to do it for us, so that we could be forgiven from all our sins, made clean and ready and able to turn to God at any moment.

God doesn't like our pain. It doesn't make Him happy. But God has given us the ability to help ourselves buy giving us the brains to come up with the amazing technology that helps predict some of these events. He has given us brains and patience to help heal another person with medicine used wisely. He has given people a gift to help others, whether that's to show others what is happening in parts of the world, or whether that's to physically help them. He has given us hearts to love them, and comfort them and fight for them.

God overpowers all the evil schemes, and will turn it to good in the end, even we don't know what that is, in our life time. Just look at Job, he goes through physical and emotional agony, but God proves to Job, and to us, that Satan will never win in the end. At the end of the Book of Job, we leave him happy and more prosperous than before! And in the meantime, He records every tear we cry, (Psalm 56:8) and promises us that when we finish our journey home, there will be no more tears, no more suffering. Just love. The battle is won!

The note from God says,

"I love you so much. You are beautiful to Me. I do not enjoy pain and suffering. I did not plan pain, although I knew it would come. When you come home to Me, there will be no pain. None. I feel your pain too. I felt it when I died on the cross. I felt it with every stroke of the whip. I felt it in every rejection, and when my friend died, or suffered and I feel it when you are in pain too. I am gentle, and I want to help you. I can help you if you let Me. Don't try to understand it, just trust that I have you in the palm of My hand. I have you. Every single one of My darling children. I have you. I am

wrapped around you in your pain. I carry you through the tough times. I am there, with you, always. The battle is raging, but you know how it will end. You know that I have won the battle. So fear not, for I am there. I will make things right, no matter what. I will not interfere with peoples choices, but I will judge them accordingly. Rest in Me. I am with you. I love you. You are mine. I will keep your heart safe. I will not break you, I will heal you."

Chapter Five

Peace be with you! We are
part of one body. No sense
in fighting with each other.

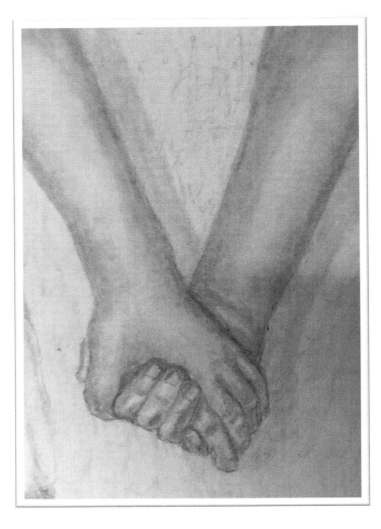

"The God of peace be with you all. Amen."
Romans 15:33 NIV UK

Peace be with you! We are part of one body. No sense in fighting with each other.

There seems to be so much unrest at the moment! There's so much fighting. It makes me sad to see people, who might otherwise be friends, hating each other. As a parent, people choosing fighting, over friendship, is something I see a fair bit! My children are mostly the best of friends, but suddenly something shifts and an argument starts. Something happens that the other did not like, or think was fair. One of them looses their patience and becomes angry with the other. An unkind comment is said, which upsets the other, and further insults follow loudly.

Do I like to watch my children argue with each other? Actually, that is something which drives me mad! I feel so disappointed that they are saying hurtful things to the other one, and so sad for the one who gets hurt. Often though, they both get hurt and I am disappointed and sad for each of them!

How do I deal with it? Not always brilliantly, I have to confess! Sometimes I intervene, and sometimes I let them fight it out. I always insist on an apology and a hug though for each other. How does God feel when His children fight? Probably much the same as I do about my children! Sad, disappointed and more than likely, quite fed up! He asks us in the Bible not to let the sun go down on an argument, to forgive each other, to love each other. Do I do that? I know He would like me to!

Let's hear some more of Carls story.

As a small lad I never really got angry that much, but did have a lot of tizzy fits. Even in my teens I would have lots of horrid thoughts, like wanting to smack someone in the mouth.

I had a friend at work, who would always calm me down, when he saw what he called the red mist! If someone was rude or back chatting or if indeed I did not like the way they spoke I'd get mad.

Also at work I had another great friend that seemed to watch my back, he knew when I was getting mad as I'd utter the words "What did you say?" Again he called it the red mist! The slightest thing would set me off. My wife, Karen, used to call it the 'Haggett Evil Streak'!

I have done a lot of things I am not proud of. To give you an example of the sort of thing I am talking about, years ago I was driving a van and Karen was in it, we got to the bottom of a road and this man just kept beeping, I said to her if he beeps again I would get out and smash him..of course he did beep and I got out walked over and whacked him in the face.

Oh and the really embarrassing ones are when I've got angry in doors and chucked my dinner on the floor and swore at my wife, a lot. It don't make me feel good now, that's for sure!

Also the thoughts I used to have, many times while in debate, the thought to hit would come into my head. While they never really ended in fists they was not far off it!

So since becoming a Christian what have I learnt? Well that it's not worth it, even if at the time you are mad but it's weird as it don't just all stop because you are a Christian, I'm finding that you have to ask God to change you and that is a long road (well for me). You see when I become a Christian, I was still the same me with the same body, mind etc. I was born again, spiritually but the rest of me was not and day by day I'm *being changed. I ask God to change my heart and my thoughts and the whole of me and He is, but it doesn't happen overnight.*

I have changed a lot though! Just a few weeks ago someone was rude to me and I said to Karen, "You know a couple of years ago," She cut me short and said, "I know!"

Sometimes I wonder how I bite my tongue I really do! It's funny, I just want to laugh now, instead of fight! Of course, I am still human and things can get too much, but what does putting someone up against a wall do? I often think what would Jesus do?

Sometimes I even wonder why I'm being so calm and don't even understand why I'm not losing it but it feels good not to.

*In the car is the big one, as that's where most of my rage kicked in, I was the worst and wanted to hurt people on what I called '**my** road' and I watch people with the same issues daily and I think, "Wow! I was like that!" Inviting Jesus in my life is the reason why, I know that, even if it makes me sound a loon bag to a lot of my friends!*

You know, going to church don't make you any more Christian, than going to the garage makes you a car. Your beliefs don't make you a better person; your behaviour does.

Your words mean nothing, if your behaviour is the complete opposite. Having true faith, in whatever it is you believe, must be shown through actions. Believing is only half the battle. Let your dreams be bigger than your fears, your actions louder than your words, and your faith stronger than your feelings.

My confrontational way has not always been the best thing for me! There have been many, many times, when I have so wished that I could come across in a lovely mild mellow way and be sooo quiet and loving, but I guess God knew that was never going to happen and I guess that's why He really did set the fire work off up my rear and jolt me in to life.

What is the note from God?
Luke 24:36 "While they were still talking about this, Jesus himself stood among them and said to them, 'Peace be with you.'"

Jesus lived a life of peace, but was seen to get very angry when people stepped away from what is right, particularly in defence of others or His Father. It's ok to be angry when something is not right, but in the appropriate way, and at the appropriate time.

When He found people turning the temple into a den of thieves, Jesus got mad, really mad! He was furious and even over turned tables. (Mark 11:15-17) So if He was allowed to get angry with people to this extent, why is it such a big deal to go mad at someone when they bug you too much? The simple answer is; Jesus didn't hurt anyone. He stood up for what is right. He raised the issue loud and clear, issues that people must have already known were a problem. Jesus pointed out the truth, showing people where they were drifting from it, or just plainly ignoring the truth. Jesus never threw a strop about someone hurting His feelings, or when He didn't get his own way, or needed to do something He couldn't be bothered to do. Jesus never pushed people out the way, punched anyone, was spiteful to them, held a grudge, yelled at anyone, or hurt them. He lived in peace. God's Peace.

He didn't get angry when people were pushing around Him wanting to see Him, or asking Him favour after favour, expecting Him to keep going hour after hour, day after day. He didn't start to resent His mate Judas when He knew he was about to send Him to a terrible death. He didn't sulk when He knew His good mate Peter, would say that he never even knew Him. He didn't fight back when they came to hurt Him. He didn't shout back when they taunted Him as they beat Him and watched Him suffer and He didn't curse them as He died on the cross. No, He forgave them. He was gentle with everyone. He angered slowly and in a righteous way. He loved them all, still.

I find that amazing. He forgave the people who had ganged up against Him, tortured him, and hung Him of a cross to die an agonizing death whilst they taunted Him! He forgave them! He forgave everyone who expected Him to help them, to fix things, His mates who hurt Him. He forgave them. He didn't hold a grudge, He just continued to love them, just as they were.

Jesus advocated peace amongst all His people, even when the guards came to take Him to His death, He stopped the fight that started and healed the wound. (Luke 22:51)

He said the words 'Peace be with you', (Luke 24:36) when He found His disciples discussing all the events after His death. They were probably feeling very upset and confused. Everything Jesus had said would happen had happened! How amazing! They were convinced that He was the son of God before He died and rose again, but now, had He really risen? Where was He? Some said they had seen Him with their own eyes. He truly is the son of God! Could this be?

Then He was there! Could it really be Him? Were they dreaming? No! Did He come charging up to them shouting 'See, here I am! I told you so!' or slapping them all on the back and congratulating Himself? No! He said 'Peace be with you.' He calmed them down, and explained what was going on. He told them to have peace.

Some dictionaries define Peace as 'freedom from war and violence, especially when people live and work together happily without disagreements'.

This is what Jesus wished for us all. Do we live in peace? I think maybe most of us fail at that most of the time! I think of all the times I get cross, and I wonder how many of those times it could be avoided! Quite a few, I have to confess!

It doesn't help me feel any better either when I am cross. In fact I feel worse and it doesn't change a thing! In fact it generally makes everything much worse! I say something that I don't actually mean, or say something I do mean, but in completely the wrong way and at the wrong time, or lose sleep over it. Perhaps this is part of the reason that we are told to let the anger go by bed time! (Ephesians 4:26)

The news reports people fighting with each other all the time! Whether it is people brawling in the streets over something that must seem, even to them, pointless afterwards, people fighting in business over money, or leaders of countries fighting for power. Not to mention the like of terrorists fighting to create fear and gain power. Why do they do it? Wouldn't it be nicer to live peacefully with each other? We are strongly encouraged throughout the Bible to love our neighbours. (Mark 12:31, Romans 13:9 and Galations 5:14, to list just a few!) So who is our neighbour? That's everyone. Not just the person next door to us!

There is no sense in fighting, with anyone. After all, these people are my brothers and sisters, and together we make up the body of the church. If you think about a car, every part is needed. Even the seemingly insignificant parts like the electric window button are important, and often these extras make the car much more expensive and desirable! The car just wouldn't be the same if a bit was missing! There is no sense hating any part of my own body, (no matter what the mirror says on a bad day!) because without that part, my body would not be complete. There is just no sense in fighting. There is just no point!

The note from God says,

*"Don't waste your time and energy in fighting.
I made each of you differently. You
complement each other. I made you for good
reasons. I made you to love each other. That
is the only way. That is the way to be happy.
Just love each other, respect each others
differences. I need and want every one of
you. I love you all. You are all worth loving.
Please love each other and let Me love and
guide you. Live in My love and I will show you
how to love others, they way I intended. You
are beautiful. I see the real you, and I love
you. I see inside each person, and I love
them all. Every single one. You are so special.
Please treat each other that way. I made
each of you for a purpose and that is enough.
Be happy with what you have, there is no
need to wish for more. Just rest in My
peace."*

Chapter Six

Growing in God.

The fruits of the Spirit.

"'I am the vine; you are the branches. If you remain in me
and I in you, you will bear much fruit; apart from me you
can do nothing."   John 15:5 NIV UK

Growing in God. The fruits of the Spirit.

There are times when I feel content to be how I am, and although I may feel an underlying desire or need to do something, I suppress it, so that I can stay in my comfort zone. It's nice in my comfort zone! It's not scary, I am safe there. But then, I wonder why I do not understand more of the Bible, or why I don't hear from God as much as others, or why I am not maturing. So why does it take me so long to move forward? Is it OK to stay as I am? Most probably not!

Would I like it if my children were lazy? Not much! I think how frustrated I get when the dishes don't make it into the dishwasher, or the rubbish into the bin! I like to teach my children to help, and help with a smile! I like them to act well when they are with others, as well as at home. They are a reflection of me, so I would like them to be seen to act appropriately! God likes us to play out our role, as His children too, and do it willingly. He made us each for a purpose, as we have seen and He wants us to produce His fruit. This will identify us as His children. It will make us different and special.

God teaches us in His Word that He wants us to follow His example. Jesus did not stay static. He expected others to teach this to the next person, and help them do the same.

Carl says he has changed a great deal since becoming a Christian and continues to notice changes.

Before the summer in 2010, every other word that I spoke was a swear word, in fact I was so bad, that I had to be careful in front of the kids. Now I don't really swear much at all!

I could be so nasty and at work! I was horrid! If people upset me, they knew about it and now I don't lose it with them at all.

I would steal from my firm to make extra money and now I won't even think about it.

I used to get road rage up to five or six times a day and now, well now, I'm teaching people to drive!

My wife says I look different, even my writing has changed!

I had a drugs problem for most of my life, on and off, and even when I thought it was gone it would come back and tempt me sometimes. Now that's dead and gone as well.

I am so happy that it scares people! When I say that, I mean that people even come up to me and ask me what I'm on and why I'm being so positive! When they ask I tell them, "It's God!"

I now pray, even though I find it really hard to do, but I do it! Before, I would only pray for greed and now I pray for others.

I've decided it's all or nothing, which means getting the crap out of my life, of course I'm no saint, but I can't help myself! At work on the Monday morning after I became a Christian, properly, my mate had, let's say, 'borrowed' a couple of things and I said "Mate, I'm not doing it." He looked at me like I was a mad man, but he knew I was serious. I told him a few bits and yes, he laughed, just like Karen said they would, but all day he said, "Stop smiling like that!" Back at the yard, another mate asked how my week was I said "Great!" and he said I have come back not as Carl! I'll just take that as a compliment!

I only ever really believed in me, before I became a Christian, and didn't really trust too many people. Now I believe in God, and most important to me now, is that I know Him more and show others.

I don't really know if all you guys believe or know, or just want to know God. I don't know because most Christian people I meet don't stand up to be counted and tell their story and I, for one, am going to put my head on the block, and tell people. I'm an Arsenal fan and I tell people about them and how I like to follow them and how I want them to do well, so I only think it fair that I tell everyone about Jesus in my life. I never thought I would be doing that, but why hide? I think too many do that already.

Since becoming a Christian, I have been different. If you have invited Jesus into your life, and you know He is there, then I believe you are truly on the path of righteousness. In Romans 3:22 and Philippians 3:9, it says righteousness comes by having faith in Jesus and not by our effort. You will no longer want to do any of the bad or sinful things in your life. Instead you can become a light for others. People want to know why you seem different. I had friends who were doing and dealing drugs, and stealing, then I no longer wanted that.

People now come up to me and ask me about God. They ask me to answer their questions and they ask me to help them. They seem to want to hear how it happened for me. I sometimes feel very small when I am talking, as I don't want it to be about me personally. It's about God, not me. God is just using me to help others, and I am happy to be used. In Luke chapter 10, the Lord tells us that the harvest is plentiful and the workers are few. We are being sent out as lambs among the wolves. I fully get this as I have felt like a lamb many times!

I also started seeing picture, images, and visions after I became a Christian as God was showing me things. I once saw rings of fire around me, then later during prayer, someone else said that they had a picture in their head of me inside rings of fire!! Weird!

I have seen images inside paintings and drawings giving me a message from God.

Recently I felt the Spirit on me really powerfully during some really great worship and I was surrounded by bright lights. I could clearly see a dark coloured bird flying away. I felt free to hold my hands out to God, (something I've never been comfortable with!) and later I was singing, and found that I was singing in tongues! It made me jump and then laugh! Someone over heard and came to me later and said it was beautiful singing! I'm not a singer, so it must have been God!

I have also felt the Holy Spirit make my legs go to jelly and lay me out! I have been overwhelmed with tears, of *joy, relief, and all emotions! The Holy Spirit it amazing! Better than drugs anytime!*

So how have I changed since becoming a Christian? What fruits do I show now? I am a lot of different things now and do things different;

I'm calmer,

I'm nicer,

I get less road rage,

I don't tell lies,

I'm a better Dad,

I'm not a thief,

I have no evil thoughts,

I'm in control of myself,

Nothing is a problem!

What is the note from God?
Galatians 5:22-23 "But the fruit of the Spirit is love, joy, peace, forbearance, kindness, goodness, faithfulness, gentleness and self-control. Against such things there is no law."

God made each of us, not to stand still, but to pass it one! He wants us to live as He wanted us to, to do things He made us to do. He does not want us to be satisfied with a little of the good things, but He wants us to want more! He wants more, from us! I don't mean that He is not happy with where we are at the moment, as we are just where He wants us, but as it says in Ecclesiastes 3:1, everything is for a season. If the weather didn't change, the leaves wouldn't turn the apple trees into their autumn splendour and allow the leaves to fall and the tree to rest, then new life begin, in an array of colourful blossom and juicy fruit in the summer.

Likening our lives to a fruit tree, the Bible says we have different types of fruit that we should be growing; love, peace, patience, forgiveness, joy, gentleness, goodness, kindness, and self control. I would love to show all these qualities! I can sometimes show one at a time, sometimes even two or three on a good day! But generally one of these fruits stumps me, (usually self control!) However we are expected to show His fruit. We are expected to grow this fruit. To do this we must keep moving! We must mature and understand. We must listen and ask questions, we must weigh and test the answers. Jesus says in John 15:4-5 that we can do nothing away from Him. He says that a branch away from the vine cannot produce fruit. He says in John 15:1, that He will prune the branches that give fruit, so that they continue to bear good fruit.

A baby apple tree produces few, if any apples, but a mature apple tree produces a vast amount of fruit, enough to feed many. We need to grow up spiritually too. As we grow we will start to notice that we are producing fruit! And the more we grow, the more fruit we will produce.

I was talking with friends about the London 2012 Olympics Opening Ceremony, and we were blown away by the symbolism of passing and the lighting of the torch. Just before the lighting of the cauldron, the older generation of athletes passed the torch to the younger generation. Each of the athletes wore a uniform to show where they were from. All the athletes were working towards a common goal. This is what God wants. He wants us to show that we belong to Him. He wants people to see that we are His people. He wants it to be obvious. Not by wearing particular clothes, but by living the life He wants us to live. We are told that we should shine like stars in the universe. (Philippians 2:15) In other words, we need to live bright, attractive lives. We need to live differently from others, to live in love. He wants us to show others how to live, and help others find God. He wants us to pass the torch. He wants us to aim towards living in love, to all strive to do this, one common goal.

I was thinking about this as I was swimming the other day. I tried hard to swim as fast as I could, timing my progress. When I reached the deep end, and turned to swim back, I noticed bubbles and mini waves in my wake, and the thought popped into my mind, that I only created this movement in the water by moving. I could see where I was going, and when I looked back, I could see where I'd been. If I continued to look back though, I would probably accidently swim out of my lane and to a different path. I need to look where I'm going and keep moving. If I stopped swimming, the water would become still eventually, and the waves would not be seen by or affect anyone else. The swim would have been wasted.

We need to grow in God. We need to show the fruits of the Spirit. We need to pass it on to others.

The note from God says

"You are how I made you to be. You have a purpose, I would like you to achieve. So would you like to take a walk with Me? Would you like to come on a journey with Me? You don't need anything except Me, and the desire to move along with Me, as I guide you. Will you help the fruit I have placed inside you grow? That fruit is so special and no one can grow it like you can. People will see Me through you. You will shine out love, you will be blessed and

a blessing to others. I will always help you grow. Read my Word, listen and learn, then you will grow and readily produce fruit. Good sweet fruit. Fruit that others need too. I will teach you, I will help you. Will you come with Me?"

Chapter Seven

Ignoring God, and then wondering why He feels so distant.

"So do not fear, for I am with you; do not be dismayed, for I am your God. I will strengthen you and help you; I will uphold you with my righteous right hand."
Isaiah 41:10 NIV UK

Ignoring God, and then wondering why He feels so distant.

Would I like it if my children ignored that I was their mother? That would hurt so much! How bad it would be if they said to me, "I just don't know you, and I definitely don't need you or want you around." I wouldn't be able to hug them, laugh with them, comfort them, or help them. I wonder if this is how God feels. I wonder if He feels sad when He sees the choices we make, without Him. I wonder if He is watching, with sadness as the consequences of our actions happen, and I wonder if He would like to intervene, but knows He is just not welcome. If this is how God feels, then if we keep refusing His company, friendship, protection and love, how can we complain when He feels so far away? How can we complain that he seems distant?

Have you ever experienced a time when God felt a million miles away? I know I have!

Carl can also identify with this feeling.

I could never understand why God didn't show up for me. At this camp, I decided to go and listen to a talk. This was the first time I stayed the whole talk. At first I thought, "Load of rubbish!" But this guy spoke some good stuff that made sense. This guy spoke so well that I had to stay and listen. I reflected a little and got the message that no matter what you have done and no matter how bad (and I've done some really bad stuff) God will still love you.

That evening I find myself sitting with my mate (who is one top honest bloke) I find myself letting off steam, as I always do, asking stupid questions and again not really getting it. He could have just said "Oh well, Carl, if that's what you think." and left it at that, but he didn't he talked and even got me asking question! One thing he said to me was "What will it take for you?" "Wow!" I thought, "That's heavy!" I went on to say that I would like an angel to come down and sit with me (yeah I know! Heavy stuff, but that's what it would take!)

My mate told me a bit of his story and I told mine a little. He told me that Jesus has a gift for us to take if we want it. We don't have to take it, but it's there for us, and it's free, but it's up to you to accept it. You gotta want it. That was a really really top night for me that I think left a big mark that would help towards the end of that week.

Over the week I saw a few things that made me wonder, I saw people talking in tongues and I didn't mind or judge, I saw people shake uncontrollably and still I never judged. I saw two people fall to the floor like a sack of spuds. After the first one, I even looked at my fist to make sure I never wacked them! It was then I was thinking, "Come on! What is this man? Give me some of this stuff!" I've seen the God channel on TV, where people do this stuff and I would say "Oh yeah? What a good act!" But this time, I was there in the middle of it, with thousands of people and this stuff was real! They had no reason to act and they were full of things and I was jealous and envious and wanted a slice like I always have but never get any. Why not?

Also on the Thursday evening, me and my friend was having a good old chat and a drink. Yet again, it was one of those where I was asking questions and my mate was jogging me along. it was about 10pm when two more mates, came over and said "Have you seen the light on the other side of your wind break?" We went round the other side and there was a mighty cross in light! We were taken back a bit! We stepped right back and it looked amazing. I looked at the lamp on the table and we could not work out how that was happening. As he said, "There you go, that's a sign!"

The following afternoon, I just thought "I've had enough of everyone else getting it and me not." I wanted just a little sniff, so I could understand, just a little. So I was walking with Daniel, my son, while he was asleep and started talking to God, saying, "Ok, I don't know how we do this, but listen, I've had enough now! I want a bit of this stuff that I've been running from and kicking down (and I've really kicked it down!) One man, the disciple Peter, denied Jesus three times, I've done it at least three thousand!" I said, "Ok, ok! Let's talk about this gift. I want it. I want to know about it." So that was that and did I expect the heavens to open? Of course not!

That night worship was tops as it had been all week and then the speaker got up. It was one of the hosts and I liked him.

He spoke about a few things and then he spoke of some male friends that he invited round for six evenings at his house. They never believed, but they turned up and tried. I could relate to that as it sounded just like me.

The speaker carried on with his talk and I felt like he was talking about me the whole hour! "Weird!" I thought. It was then he asked for anyone who has been the whole week but who still got nothing to come up and for the first time in the week I was off up the front! I barged past everyone and I was first there, because I wanted to and because for the first time I believed God was calling me. Yes, loads went up, but I heard Him. Three different people prayed round me and it was nice.

I went back to my seat but before I even sat down, the speaker said, "Now I'm calling anyone that needs healing." "Crap!" I thought, "That's me again! My ear maybe? I can get my ear fixed." "No Carl!" I hear my friend say, "It's something else!" Anyway, I go up and this man told me he was a vicar for 30 years and asked what he could pray for so I said "My ear, as I'm deaf and that's why I've come up." He does this, but then we both look at each other and we both know it's got nothing to do with the ear! He asks me what's up, so I tell him, "I don't get it! I don't get none of it and I'm angry! Why everyone else? After all the whole week I've heard speakers say be greedy and want it and I do, but I'm not getting it!" This man was great! He never pushed me away, but instead said the same thing as my mates! Three times now and now it's getting freaky! So he said "You want to do it?"

"What have I got to do?" I said.

He said "We will pray," to which I said,

"Mate, I've never done it, and don't know what to do."

Was I scared? Bet your ass I was!

But I thought "No more running. No more fighting. I'm here now let's do this thing."

I prayed with this man and said lots of things, inviting Jesus in and getting the crap out. We spoke about the years of drug taking and other bad things that were blocking Jesus and he never judged me. He encouraged me. We did this together. He had me holding my hand out, which is one thing I would never do, but was there doing it in front of thousands of people!

He said to me after, "If anything happens, tell someone!" So I'm telling you lot, and I told my whole church when I got back!

God used that speaker to get through to me, as I went back to my seat the first time. It was like God smiling, saying "WHAT! Where are you going? You've still not got it! Get back up to the front!" So he used the speaker to tempt me back there, with me thinking it was to heal my deafness. I bet God thought, "That will get him back up to the front!" And it did! But I and God and the vicar, (oh, and my friend) knew it wasn't for that!

I went back to my seat and felt glad I done it. It was then I flicked a moth from my hair and it was less than a foot from me and it vanished! (Believe me! I've not done L.S.D. for 20 years, so it was real!) I said to Karen, "Did you see that?"

"No," she said.

Weird! Don't know what that meant!

On the Friday evening, we all met for a drink and I was quite quiet. I was just reflecting, but you know when something is different in you.

On the Saturday we went home and I was helping to unload van, when this birds nest fell from a tree right in front of me! Again I thought "What is this?" it was like I was being told chuck all the old things out.

The Sunday morning, again was weird! I always buy thick bacon where you get six rashers in a pack, and I've got six in a pack for the last six years but that day there was seven! I thought that was God saying to me "That's for free mate! Take it as it's yours!"

In the service on the Sunday, the talk was about the story of Jacob. My friend said to me "Funny! He was talking about him as he was always fighting God, just like you!"

My mocking of God and inviting him in, and not meaning it was, the reason I never got it! It was only when I was hungry and really wanted God did he come to me.

Thousands of people can show you the door but only you can walk through it.

That was it but then on Sunday evening I showed Karen what I wrote for the church about my week, and she comes over with her Bible, saying, "Look! I had this for you, it is Matthew 7:7 Ask, Seek, Knock." But she got a shock when she saw what was after that; the narrow and wide gates, she said it was what I was saying, about thousands can show you the gates but only you can walk through it.

So what has the best bit about stopping denying God and inviting Him in?

You know what the best bit is? All of it!

The seeing

The visions

The understanding the Bible

The not being blind and deaf anymore to God,

The knowing that your whole world can be changed.

Not wanting to do bad things.

The knowing that all the bad things that you ever done in your whole life have been lifted up and God said, "Carl, you are a new man. All this is done, gone chucked away."

I can't just name one bit, but my wife sums it up, when she says to me, for the first time, she feels free. That made me sad at first (well for 5 seconds) but I know what she means.

Jesus can come in to your life, like He has with mine, and change your whole life. But you still have the old body, and that takes a little while to change, but believe me, it does.

Please don't think for one second that I am a saint as I'm far from that. It's been a road of fifteen years for me, knocking it all and thinking it was all rubbish, to being here today putting my head on the block. Since 2010, I have had loads of changes and I now get to see lights around people heads and get pictures and words and I used to think people were off their heads that said that!

People ask me if I still do things that I should not. Yes, of course! Then, you may ask "What's the point then?" The point is that I don't want to do anything that I shouldn't and I am now a lot more in control. The point is also, that when you become a Christian and really mean it and have truly taken Jesus into your life, that you really don't want to be doing silly or bad things and if you do its weird and it makes you feel sick, whereas before, I didn't really care.

So what is letting God in like?

Two words… life changing………if you want it to be…..

So what is the note from God?

John 14:16-18 "And I will ask the Father, and he will give you another advocate to help you and be with you forever – the Spirit of truth. The world cannot accept him, because it neither sees him nor knows him. But you know him, for he lives with you and will be in you. I will not leave you as orphans; I will come to you.'"

God wants to live in us. He wants to be close to us. He wants to be there with us, every moment, of every day and night. Before He went to the cross for us, Jesus was talking to His disciples. He was trying to reassure them that although they wouldn't be able to see Him anymore, He would not leave them (John 14:18).

John 14:16 says that He would send the Holy Spirit, the 'Spirit of Truth' as He is described in John 14:17, who will be with us, in us, filling us. He has sent His Spirit to live in us, defending us, helping us, helping us talk to God heart to heart, when we don't know what to say, giving us amazing power (Acts 1:8), giving us amazing gifts (1 Corinthians 12:7-11), and guiding us, always.

I don't want to turn that kind of friend down! I want to invite the Spirit in completely and ask Him to stay! I don't want to deny myself that kind of friend!

Often though, I notice that people do deny Him. I can see that people push Him away, wanting to do things their own way, but then get angry when they can't feel God.

God wants to be close to us. All of us! Jesus likens him to a shepherd, who would make sure the whole flock were safe, always. A shepherd who, if one little sheep were to wander away, would secure the rest, where they are, leave them and search tirelessly until he found the stray sheep and had returned it to the flock. (Luke 15:3-6)

In Luke 15:11-31, Jesus talks about a son who was given free reign, and abused it. The father of this boy must have been heartbroken as he could only watch as his child made stupid mistake after stupid mistake, even ending up homeless and eating food meant for pigs. He must have been so desperate to help in any way he could, but known that the boy must make his own choices in order to mature, learn and grow. That must have taken some doing! I don't know how long I could bite my tongue and watch from a distance as my children made so many painful mistakes.

So did the boy learn? Yes! He made a decision to come home and beg for forgiveness. As he returned, his father was delighted to see him in the distance, and saw his son's heart had changed. He saw that his son was ready to listen and allow himself to be guided in his choices. He saw that his little boy was ready to ask for help, gain wisdom and accept love and guidance from his loving father.

Whilst his son who had caused so much heartache was still a long way off, the father came running to him. He welcomed him lovingly and joyfully held him close. He didn't wait for his son to come all the way to him, or even half way; he was still a long way off and the father came to him.

I find this very comforting, in that I know when I have messed up, and messed up in a big way, that my Heavenly Father will always welcome me back. All I need to do is to turn back to him, with a changed heart, and a heartfelt apology, and He will meet me there. That's what to repent means: to have a change of heart. To change my mind that my ways that I had been thinking were right, were in fact wrong and admit this and turn back to the right path.

It says in the Bible, in Psalm 103:12, that the Father removes our sin as far "as from east is from west." I love this verse, as it makes me realise that it's never too late to come back to God, no matter what we've done. He is there knocking and waiting for us to answer the door, (Matthew 7:7) As I said in the very beginning of this book, He will not barge in, He will always wait to be invited. Once He is invited, then our relationship can start, or start all over again. He can point us in the right direction, help us find peace, help us be who He made us to be. Then we will know that He is not distant and no matter what is happening, it will work out for good in the end.

Let's go back to the lost son. What about the other son, the son who had been sensible, and who had held the fort whilst his flaky, irresponsible brother had been out partying? Was he thrilled when his brother returned? Probably initially, but then as his father lavished luxury on him and threw a huge party, it made him feel a little put out to say the least! He questions his father about this, who simply says, my son who was lost, is now found! I hope the brother understood. I can only think of my own children and put myself in the fathers place. If one of my children had made some bad choices, and I thought they were lost but then they came back, I would be overjoyed too! I would run out to them and throw my arms round them, probably with more than a few tears too! I would celebrate their return and I would expect the other child to celebrate with me too. I would recognise that they had been good and loyal, but I would also celebrate that the lost and found child had turned away from a life of unhealthy, dangerous choices and towards me who loves them and healthy, safe choices and I would help them on this path, in any way I could.

This makes me smile. It makes me smile, that if we stop denying God, and invite Him in, God will meet us where we are, and help us on our path back to Him, and back to a healthy life. The life, that, He meant for us.

The note from God says,

"I am not distant. I am right there. Always. No matter what's been going on, no matter when you call, no matter where you are. All you have to do is let Me in. I will do the rest! I will meet you where you are. I will always welcome you with open arms. I can't wait for you to call Me! I have been waiting for you to turn towards Me just a little, then let me hug you. I can't wait to hold you close and help you feel how much I love you. For I do love you! So much! Before you were even born, I planned every single one of your days. I knew which choices you would make, and I knew that one day I would be able to walk with you, One day I would be able to have you sit on my knee and snuggle right in, listening to the sound of My heartbeat, whilst I gently hold you close, comforting and soothing you. I

have been with you your whole life. I have been there in the best times, and through the hardest times, and some of those times have been so hard haven't they? I want to be there more and more for you. I want to wrap myself around you and gaze at you with all the love in Me. I know that is overwhelming, but please know, I am always with you. I will always love you. Always. I love you and I will never leave you. I will always welcome you back into My loving arms."

**So there are the Seven notes from God.
So what's next?**

If you have read God's words written just for you, and felt something stir inside you, I would encourage you to sit with Him for a while.

I would encourage you to pray a simple prayer, inviting Him in, accepting His Son Jesus Christ who died for you. You could pray and ask for, and accept, His forgiveness. You could ask to let Him wrap himself around you and to fill you completely with His Holy Spirit, healing and comforting you, and helping your wisdom grow.

I would encourage you to find your Bible and dust it off, or download an app of the Bible and ask God to teach you. A word or verse, or chapter might just help right now.

I would encourage you to call into your local church and chat to someone. I would encourage you to tell a friend.

I will be praying for you.
In His love, Sarah x

Just as you are

Just as you are, you are lovely to me,

Just as you are, I don't see what you see.

Just as you are, I love you so much.

Just as you are, imperfections and such.

Just as you are, who I loved to create,

Just as you are, the one I celebrate.

Just as you are, you are pleasing to me,

Just as you are, your beauty I see.

Sarah Parrott

122

References

I have used some resources to help me write this book.
They are listed below if you would like to read them
yourself.

NIV Bible (UK version)
Bible Gateway http://www.biblegateway.com/
Cambridge dictionary:
http://dictionary.cambridge.org/dictionary/british
Pictures by Sarah Parrott